YOUR MONEY
MENTALITY

YOUR MONEY MENTALITY

HOW YOU FEEL ABOUT RISK, LOSSES, AND GAINS

J. TED OAKLEY

RIVER GROVE
BOOKS

Published by River Grove Books
Austin, TX
www.rivergrovebooks.com

Distributed by River Grove Books

Design and composition by Greenleaf Book Group and Mimi Bark
Cover design by Greenleaf Book Group and Mimi Bark

Publisher's Cataloging-in-Publication data is available.

Print ISBN: 978-1-63299-427-1

eBook ISBN: 978-1-63299-428-8

First Edition

Oxbow Advisors

At Oxbow Advisors, we've spent thirty-five years working with people who have gained significant first-generation wealth and are trying to maximize it across future generations.

Many of these individuals have experienced liquidity events, and they depend on our extensive knowledge to help them navigate the next steps that will lead to lasting, cross-generational wealth.

What we do is simple, but hard to find in today's investment world: We protect the wealth you worked hard to create.

If you would like more information, call 512-386-1088
or visit www.oxbowadvisors.com

CONTENTS

*Important: If you do not have time to read this entire book, please make sure you read the "Regrets" section in Chapter 8 and the "If You Only Ask One Question" section in the Conclusion.
—Ted Oakley

Know Thyself

There's nothing like an economic crisis to test the mettle and show investors' true colors.

Case in point: In the early wake of the 2020 pandemic, I had two wealthy investors sell everything on the very bottom day of the year. Frustrated, confused, and desperate, they panicked and ducked out. Investing is never for the faint-hearted, but it's moments like those when you learn—often far too late—what kind of risk tolerance you really have and how that should be impacting your investment choices.

At Oxbow Advisors, many of our investors come to us after experiencing life-changing liquidity events. They've sold a business, been bought out by partners, retired and cashed out, or come into newly liquid wealth in other ways. The thing most have in common is that they've been extremely successful at some endeavor, made a fortune, and now they're looking to be equally successful as investors. This is not something that happens automatically. Why would it? Being good at golf doesn't mean you're good at baseball. They're two completely different games—and so are business management and wealth management.

One of the biggest and most glaring pitfalls new investors face is not knowing their own money mentality, especially when it comes to risk. They don't have enough experience to know their comfort level, and so they make mistakes like buying aggressively at the top, selling in desperation at the bottom, and—the cardinal sin—leveraging funds that should be set aside for long-term peace of mind.

Things don't have to play out this way. Investors can do better. One of the biggest steps in the right direction is taking time to make an honest assessment of your risk tolerance. Chances are, it's a more complicated issue than it seems on the face of things.

It's been more than two thousand years since the maxim *Know Thyself* was inscribed on the Temple of Apollo. The words and the sentiment have been echoed by philosophers ever since— from Aristotle and Plato to Benjamin Franklin and Ralph Waldo Emerson. There are few areas where the consequences of not heeding this ancient advice are more immediate or dire than in the world of investment, where fortunes made over decades can dwindle away over days if you've over- or underestimated your tolerance for volatility.

In the chapters that follow, we'll explore common investor profiles, types of risk, a number of angles you need to consider in your self-assessment, and what steps you can take to ensure that the guidance you're receiving matches your priorities. Risk tolerance is at the heart of most money decisions, and learning to know yourself will make you a better investor and a better partner for the people you trust to give you financial guidance.

CHAPTER 1

Four Volatility Types

Over the course of 40 years here at Oxbow we've developed a good sense for identifying investor types. Surprisingly, most people fall into one of just a few categories of risk tolerance. When investors are at one extreme or the other (either can't accept risk at all or can't stay away from it) I know we're going to have a hard time making them happy. Here's why: Investing is not strictly linear, and successful investing is rarely a matter of all or nothing. In its own way, it's an art—part data science, part research, part experience, part emotion and intuition. There are times when the practice of that art boils down to making counterintuitive choices, even though going a different way than the crowd is a real challenge for some people.

Investing inevitably has highs and lows, and those are the times investors discover their risk tolerance may be different from what it seemed when they were weighing hypotheticals. Responses to actual gains and losses are powerful and emotional. Knowing this can help you choose to be careful and deliberate in stating your risk tolerance. Instead of defaulting to what you think it should be, sit with questions on this topic for a while. Consider what a high or low tolerance will mean in both best- and worst-case situations.

There are a lot of factors that play into where each investor lands on the risk-comfort continuum, but one that's a pretty consistent predictor is the time period in which they were raised. People who went through the Great Depression were never comfortable with stocks because they saw so many go broke in the market. People who came up through the 70s and early 80s are inclined to be conservative and worry about inflation. People who were coming of age in the late 80s tend to like stocks because they went up and up during those years. Our younger investors today—the group born from the early 1980s to the early 2000s and dubbed *millennials* by authors and generational theorists Neil Howe and William Strauss—have seen two extremes of investing. From 1982-2000, many were watching their parents thrive in the great bull market. Then they saw major bear markets from 2000-2003 and 2008-2009. On the periphery of their childhoods and college years, fortunes were being made and lost, sometimes very publicly. Their observations caused many of this group to be a little wary of the market and to have a greater appreciation for cash.

Another great predictor is the type of family in which a person grows up. This often has a profound influence on investing preferences in adulthood. For a child who grew up wanting nothing, risk can come easily. And why not? Money has always been a reliable friend and they expect nothing bad will happen. For a child who grew up poor or wanting though, there's often a tendency to be more careful and conservative, and to abhor the idea of losing money. This phenomenon is especially interesting because many people are not aware that they have this tendency.

Beyond basic demographics, these are some of the personality types I've seen time and again over my long investment advising career:

Nervous Ned: At their core, this is a person who does not do well with loss. For them, the fear of losing is stronger than the positive feelings associated with coming out ahead. One of the big issues in this group is that Neds are prone to panicking and pulling the plug. They may tell me in a meeting that they're ok with some risk, that they know long-term growth will come, but that's not really what they mean. As soon as they see a loss, they pull out. Their money mentality won't let them go there. They worry most about taking a loss.

Clearly, this volatility type doesn't lend itself to stocks. Many of these individuals are only comfortable with CDs, or they require investments they can constantly see and control. This does not make them bad business people. In fact, they may be great at buying companies or real estate. The worst circumstances occur when people in this group are not self-aware until they're watching stocks and bonds move around and realizing they have zero tolerance for the way that makes them feel. If they'd known their money mentality, many might never have started a stock fund at all, because any competent financial advisor would have warned them stocks inevitably do go down at some point—even if they will eventually come back.

The sad fact is a lot of investors who fit this profile only learn the hard way. Their literal, physical style of learning requires them to see loss to believe it exists. They kick the tires on investments, smell the wood floors at the bank, eyeball paper account statements—all material experiences. Many of these people come from physical businesses that helped make them so solely focused on tangibles. Investment-wise, this can make them one-trick ponies who may only see modest returns, but that's okay. It's better to know who you are and where you place your priorities as you make your investment decisions than it is to find out after you've been hit with a loss—even a temporary one—that you can't handle.

Fomo Fred: This is a person who always sees the glass half full. They have an optimistic attitude that everything is pointing up, especially stock prices. They're always a little (or a lot) afraid of missing out, and their best days are the ones when they can tell a friend how they made a killing on a stock. These are people who love the excitement of the markets. They get a contact high from a rapidly climbing stock (examples from my career include Coca-Cola running up from $1.50 to $12 in the 80s, Cisco climbing from $1 to $80 in the 90s, and, more recently, Apple and Amazon rocketing from $12 to $290 and $50 to $3000 respectively). Who wouldn't enjoy that ride?

Reality check: Most stocks don't take the express elevator to the top, and even when they do, it always eventually goes back down. This is the flaw in Fred's *always be in it* approach. You may remember the old joke about the optimistic boy who looks at a pile of manure and remarks, *There must be a pony in there somewhere.* That's the bullish-all-the-time mentality of this investor type—except it doesn't reveal the fear of missing out that motivates these individuals. When an aggressive investor is primarily fueled by any type of fear—even of being left behind—that's an indicator that the enthusiasm is hiding a more risk-averse true self.

People in this group have such an innate drive toward always making more that it overshadows their decisions. They often make poor choices, especially feeling like they need to jump in, buying at the top (sometimes repeatedly). They worry most about missing an opportunity.

I have studied this group for many years and tried to determine their mental makeup. In many cases, they come from families where they never had to worry about money. That sets the stage for confidence in future outcomes. In many ways that attitude is a godsend, but in investing it can really get a person into trouble. Even if they connect with conservative money managers who try to steady their hands, they eventually leave because they want to be fully in it to win it. They have no fear . . . right up until the investments take a substantial drop. That's the point at which Freds often do the very worst thing—they sell at a low, start seeing their former holdings climbing back up, and experience FOMO all over again. It's a vicious and dangerous pattern.

What should they have done? Easy. Pick an investment they can live with in volatile times and leave the rest of their assets in safety. That way they can enjoy the big upswings and weather the downs, always knowing they have plenty in their shelter accounts.

Have-It-All Jane: This is a person who combines the greatest vulnerabilities of both Neds and Freds. She is highly uncomfortable with risk while at the same time eager to pursue a high return. This is a person who doesn't want to lose any money, who may panic about it, but who can't stand to miss out on anything. Most are looking for a 10%-plus return, and they mistakenly believe that's possible without taking chances. They worry equally about losing and not making enough.

This group of people who expect great profits with little risk are constantly looking for the Holy Grail money manager—the one who can make money no matter what. Not surprisingly, these are the toughest investors to deal with. Their money mentality is just not on solid ground. They live in a dream world. If they had their own business or had family assets that were completely controllable, they probably got used to having a linear type of investment return. It was easy when they sold widgets that businesses needed and consistently, endlessly bought. All they had to do was manage their people and their balance sheet and income statements.

In the public markets, these same people always have an ear or eye out for the next best thing. They complain loudly and often that they don't make enough in up markets, and they complain bitterly in down markets when they lose along with the rest of the stock-investing universe. When they gain 20% and someone else gained 21%, they aren't satisfied. When they lose 10% while the market loses 18%, they wonder why they lost at all.

My advice to the have-it-all group is this: Stop obsessing. Your money mentality is convoluted and detrimental to your financial and emotional health. Decide where you want to be and how much risk you can actually live with, then put an end to the perfectionist rant. Otherwise, you'll spend the rest of your life changing managers and being unhappy with all of them. You might even apply this philosophy in other areas of your life, because in 40 years of advising, I've seen this particular mentality carry over into professional and personal relationships and even matters of self-esteem. Human nature does not change a lot, but recognizing the detrimental effect this money mentality is having can enhance both your investments and your life.

Steady Ed: Back in the 1960s, Mr. Ed was a famous television character who happened to be a talking horse. His claim to fame (besides the obvious one) was the steady, sound advice he always gave his owner. In investment terms, Steady Eds are people who truly know themselves and their money mentality. They live with a healthy dose of fear, but they know what they want to do and that there is inherent risk. They understand the amounts of risks and rewards they want to pursue, and they clearly convey their priorities to their advisors. They know their investments, and know how to keep their emotions between the lines.

Because these individuals have established and work within an investment framework that matches their money mentality, they don't panic or feel compelled to chase the market. If something is working well, they have the ability to let it be until they see the madness that always comes from investments with a long run of success. If something is down in price, they have the ability to understand why they did it in the first place and let time do its thing. They have a complete sense of what kind of money should be in each category: cash, stocks, real estate, private business, etc. They recognize a sales pitch when they see one. They neither see the glass half full nor half empty; they just see the glass. If this group could teach money mentality, every investor could learn something.

Not surprisingly, investors in this group are usually the most successful, especially when you look at their long term outcomes.

If you fall into this category, you're a well-adjusted investor, and your money worries don't keep you up at night.

SO YOU THINK YOU'RE STEADY?

The vast majority of the investors we see at Oxbow do not come to us as Steady Eds, though many of them think they are. That's a big problem, because by the time they realize they were wrong about their comfort level with risk, it is typically too late to change it—the day they have their first big setback or significant loss. Those are the watershed moments, and too often they're the ones when investors realize there were important conversations they needed to have *before* making decisions about their money.

Steadiness plays another role as well. Overwhelmingly, people with money derive a critical sense of wellbeing by knowing they can control their lives at all times. Sudden market debacles can rapidly undermine that confidence. Investors need to be able to sleep at night, and that means being realistic about themselves and their money mentality.

In the real world, scenarios develop sooner or later to test even the wisest and luckiest investor's concept of steadiness. A few come to mind: a global stock dive when everything goes down; a poorly-timed entry (like when markets are at an all-time high just before a big swoon); or choosing investment options that look good but don't have the substance to back them up. Texans have a saying about those kinds of investments and the people who peddle them, referring to cowboys who are all hat and no cattle.

When investors get caught out in these situations, many beat themselves up unmercifully. They can't believe they were not prepared, especially because most of the people in this group are not accustomed to any kind of failure.

Too often it takes this kind of almost tragic loss on a first mistake to wake investors up. After that, they start to know who they really are and what kind of priorities they need to set for their finances.

OXBOW NOTE

For a free copy of my book **You Sold Your Company** *and more about these theories and experiences, contact us at OxbowAdvisors.com.*

CHAPTER 2

Why Does This Happen?

Most people who make it to the top by building successful ventures have a few personality traits in common. They're determined, optimistic, driven, and confident. Not surprisingly, some take those traits one step too far and get headstrong, overconfident, and aggressive in some of their choices. In my book *$20 Million and Broke*, I discuss a lot of the mistakes these people make and ways to avoid them. For those making decisions about newly liquid wealth, one of the first steps in successfully navigating the first years is remembering that true success will take *two* forms. First, you'll get that hard-earned cash-out. Second, you'll figure out a way to keep it.

If you don't understand your money mentality, you're positioned to fail at that second measure.

You may be wondering how or why on earth you'd fail to hang on to something you've already got. After witnessing countless spectacular failures over my decades in the financial world, I assure you plenty of people find ways to do just that.

There are a couple of scenarios that present themselves over and over again.

In the first, investors who are overconfident with their newly liquid cash assume they've got it all figured out. They don't seek or heed advice. They don't fear any kind of failure. They feel they've reached a *game over* point in their lives, where they can do no wrong.

Here's the truth: Having wealth in a business and investing that wealth do not require the same strengths and skills. One is an enterprise you build from scratch, creating equity and income along the way. The other is a way of preserving and growing equity you already have. Being great at one doesn't qualify you at all to do the other.

In the second scenario, investors make critical decisions based on things like dinner-party advice (or the recommendation of a friend, or something they read in the Sunday paper that gave them an inkling). It is shocking how often this happens—not on a small scale, but with millions and tens of millions of dollars on the line on a tip or a hint or a hunch.

The reality check on that: No competent business owner would dream of going out and committing to pay a vendor a quarter or third or half the worth of their company without knowing who's running the show, what they're going to make with it, how they're going to do it, what their guiding principles are, whether they've been successful in the past, and whether they are trustworthy. Odds are, that would just be a start on the due diligence that would go into the decision. And yet a large percentage of those same individuals, a few years on—after the sale of the company—don't hesitate to take $5 million or $40 million and throw it down in front of Goldman Sachs instead of taking the time to choose a competent guide, dig deep on strategy, and really think about their money mentality.

KNOW YOUR BIAS

People behave differently in day-to-day life than the ways any algorithm or investment expert can predict. The reason is simple: Money is a deeply emotional topic. It can tee up bouts of hope, greed, and joy—and just as easily spin them into panic, despair and regret. The emotional nature of investment frequently creates blind spots and even subconscious drives that sway critical decisions.

Knowing your own biases can help you stay on track. At Oxbow, we routinely see a few of these that every investor should consider and remember.

The first is *confirmation bias,* which affects individual investors and sometimes professional ones as well. In short, this bias is the tendency to interpret evidence as proof of a theory. We all do it from time to time with glass-half-full assumptions, but when you start looking for facts that support your own conclusions, you're letting it interfere with your clarity of thought. This kind of bias is particularly dangerous in the investment world, as it's possible for people with limited experience and knowledge in the field to perceive almost any bit of data as a positive if they try.

The particular danger of confirmation bias is that the more an individual wants something, the more they may find ways to justify it. Only when things really fall apart do they realize their view was skewed.

The second type of bias we frequently encounter is *ambiguity aversion* bias, an economics reference to a preference for known risks over unknown risks.

In a nutshell, this is the provenance of people who don't deal well with uncertainty. They like steady as you go—so much that they're willing to overlook and deny change to keep it that way. Unfortunately, financial markets change and evolve over time with trading, products, and systems changing from year to year, month to month, and sometimes even day to day. When it comes to money, many people don't accept new practices easily. These are the ones who, in the interest of feeling secure, tend to question or even flat-out deny change.

An easy example is in the fluctuation of interest rates. In 1982, I'd been in the investment business for 6 years. During that time, interest rates had gone up with inflation. A 30-year

US treasury bond was paying 14 percent, guaranteed. The escalation of that inflation had much of the investment world assuming those rates would stay high. It took nearly 10 years of declines for people to really start believing—even considering—that rates could keep falling. Fast forward to today and we have the opposite issue: Nobody believes that rates can go up. In order to guard against investment blunders related to either of these assumptions, you'd have to accept that rates are constantly in flux.

The *Dunning-Krueger Effect* is another bias, one in which unskilled individuals judge their ability to be much higher than it actually is relative to the people around them. This presumption of being the smartest person in the room, regardless of the subject, is where the money mentality issue shows up in an unfortunate way. Most Oxbow investors and prospective investors are objectively successful. There's no disputing that. They've sold businesses, made lots of money, and earned the respect and admiration of their peers and employees. They've *made* it.

All of that is truly worthy of celebration, but it sometimes translates to individuals wrongly convinced they've got the Midas touch—that success in one venture virtually guarantees success in the next. This kind of overconfidence can cost you dearly.

Only after you've taken a step back from the full-force charge towards your next conquest can you begin to recognize your money mentality and pursue appropriate investments to match it.

One last bias is all about *relativity*. Greed in the investment world is a tricky subject, because drive is an asset and none of our high-net-worth investors got where they are without striving. That said, it is all too easy for an individual—especially a successful one—to be so focused on gains that it overtakes everything else. The drive to outpace and out-earn everybody else has been the downfall of far too many wealthy investors. Many can't seem to be satisfied with their results, even when those results are excellent. They keep driving for more and even more. Are you like this? If so, you will be a frustrated investor for a long, long time.

The "trick" to overcoming all these biases isn't a trick at all. It boils down to things you probably learned in grade school: Be humble. Pay attention. Ask questions. Do your homework.

And then there's the one you learned in business: Seek experienced and honest guidance.

OXBOW NOTE

In my book $20 Million and Broke, *I outline the reasons wealth loss is so common in detail and with real-life examples. If you'd like a complimentary copy of this book or any of my other titles, contact us at OxbowAdvisors.com.*

CHAPTER 3

Understanding Where You Come From

Are you cautious or overconfident? In love with your wealth or burdened by it? Do you feel guilty or insecure about it? Do you think it defines who you are? Do you think it makes you a better person or that it corrupts you? No matter how much you have, do you stay up nights worrying you'll lose it? Or devising potentially risky plans to get more?

It takes time and experience to get a handle on your emotional relationship with money, and getting to the bottom of it can be tricky—kind of like asking people who they love most, the spouse or the kids.

There are ways to get at your true money mentality that you

can accomplish without having to endure a major financial wipe-out, but most people don't bother. They go about their business until their stocks plummet or the housing market crashes or, as we've seen lately, a worldwide political or medical crisis erases tens of millions of jobs and billions of investment dollars.

How can you get a handle on this *before* you get in the weeds? Consider these factors:

- *Family Priorities.* No matter what your money mentality, if it is incongruent with that of your spouse, that poses a significant problem for your family and your advisors. Whatever compromise you need to make, it has to fit the both of you—and it has to fit with your legacy plans as well. This is not an issue to be a maverick on. If something happens to you, your partner should not be blindsided by the discovery that you were gambling with assets he or she believed were earmarked for long-term security. With this in mind, figure out a way to compromise and get on the same page as soon as possible.

- *Size Matters.* One of the most important factors to consider is what you have to lose. The money mentality of people with smaller fortunes is much more acute than those with comparably large ones. If one investor has $1.5 million and another has $50 million, their mentalities are naturally going to be different. When the party with the smaller sum loses 30%, it's devastating. They can't afford it and should not have risked it. For the wealthier investor, the risk may be worth the reward, but only if they can comfortably weather it.

- *What's Your Number?* How much of your wealth is expendable in the short term? When people get financially impaired for extended periods of time, the experience has tremendous emotional consequences. Every investor should exercise enough restraint to ensure they don't get put into a position they can't weather through a bear market.

- *All Your Eggs.* Everybody knows a wise investor doesn't put all their money on one horse (though of course that doesn't keep some people from doing it). There's a related factor many people disregard, because entry point can be nearly as important. No matter what money mentality you have, if you start at the top of a 10-year up market, then you are tainted from the start and could be playing catch-up for years. This comes down to a lot more than luck, because there's never a good time to take your whole nest egg and throw it at the market in the belief it can only go up. At Oxbow, we start slow with new investors, knowing a major fluctuation could mess them up for life if they go all in. It takes knowledge and especially experience to recognize when things are cheap and when they are high. Your investment starting point can end up weighing heavily on your psyche. You need to approach it in a measured way.

- *Is Cash Flow Needed?* One of the biggest determining factors in your money mentality is whether you require cash flow from your investments. If you are dependent on cash flow, you automatically become more sensitive to risk and reward. When you have outside cash flow, you don't have to be as sensitive to levels and volatility of investments.

Over the years, we at Oxbow have noticed that investors who use cash flow from investments as a primary income source get real nervous in down markets. That is specifically and especially why you need to know your mentality if this is your situation. When a breakdown in prices comes, it'll be too late to make changes. When people say they have a high tolerance for risk, what they are really saying is that they have a high tolerance when they're making money. Few can say the same when they're losing. The problem with needing cash flow is that it demands a system that pays the investor, but also one that grows like the market—something that doesn't exist.

The other thing to keep in mind on cash flow is the ever-changing interest rate environment. For example, fifteen years ago what you would have received from investing $1 million in US Treasury bonds was $40,000. To receive that much today, you'd need to invest $3.4 million. Adjustments have to be made to current circumstances, and the investor who is mired in a model that worked in the past is especially vulnerable to failure.

OXBOW NOTE

If you recently sold your business, you're as vulnerable to wealth loss as you'll ever be in your life. For a free copy of my book Danger Time: The Two-Year Red Zone After Selling Your Company *and more books and videos on this subject, visit OxbowAdvisors.com.*

CHAPTER 4

Many Forms of Investment Risk

Investors inherently think that they understand investment risk. You buy stocks and they go up or down. You buy bonds and they pay interest on your money. Those are two basic tenets, but they barely scratch the surface. Let's talk about the rest of the story—less obvious types of risk. Far too many investors think they already understand this area when they're missing critical information.

MARKET RISK. . .

Stocks. Yes, they fluctuate—and yes, they always will. In addition, they will come and go with the economy. Most people understand this one because they see it all the time.

INTEREST RATE RISK. . .

This is an interesting one because if you have been investing for 38 years or less, you have never seen interest rates go up for any period of time. It's basically been downhill for all those years. That's a problem. We will eventually see higher rates, and when it happens investors won't know what to do. As an example, in the late 80s, an investor came into my office with bonds purchased in the late 1960s or early 70s. They may have had a 5% coupon payment, but they were priced at 60 cents on the dollar. Inflation had killed them. This may be a real risk in the next 10-15 years.

CURRENCY. . .

Since countries and economies are tied together now in a way they've never been before, there is always a risk of losing money in the exchange rates of foreign currencies. Wall Street would have you purchase all kinds of international investments, but forget to tell you about the risk that you may lose money if the dollar goes down.

LIQUIDITY RISK. . .

This is one of the greatest hidden risks in investments, and most investors pass it by when times are good. But when times are bad, liquidity becomes extremely important. If you can't sell something, then it doesn't make sense to assume it's an instant investment. It might as well be real estate. In fact, real estate might be better.

Also, when liquidity dries up, Wall Street will take advantage of you and give you the worst bid prices around.

CONCENTRATION RISK. . .

When you own too much of one thing, your risk is obviously higher. If you own your private company, that's one thing, but for public companies, moderation is key. I have seen more mistakes from investors in owning too much of one stock than almost anything else. They fall in love or they think they're hitching to a rising star and they can't get enough. Really? How about Kodak in the 1960s or Levitz Furniture in the 70s or Circuit City in the 80s? Even throw in Cisco in the 1990s. All of these were great to own for 5-8 years, but never regained their status or—even worse—went broke. I've been warning against this risk for decades, but inexperienced investors still get caught up in it all the time.

CREDIT RISK. . .

The risk that an entity or company cannot pay you when a bond comes due is real. You are loaning money, pure and simple. I dare say very few wealth managers really understand credit risk. They depend solely on a credit rating and have no idea of the other risks surrounding it. Credit risk and liquidity risk go hand in hand. A bond is a loan and you need to view it that way. Rarely do I meet retail types of investment people who understand interest coverage or demographics in municipal and corporate bonds. We have a whole generation of people who are supposed to understand credit risk, and yet they only buy exchange traded funds and have no idea what is inside them.

INFLATION RISK. . .

Retaining the purchasing power of your money is by far the Holy Grail of making it last a lifetime. I have told investors for many, many years that their primary objective should be ensuring their money retains its buying power over time, without eroding principle. Inflation cuts to the very basics of investing, because it can render today's money less valuable tomorrow. This is one of the reasons putting all your assets into fixed-rate investments is a recipe for disaster. If inflation hits 7% but your money is only earning 4%, you've got a problem that gets worse every day. One of the ways to offset this is with the value of hard assets, but even those can be vulnerable. Many of today's investors have never witnessed inflation. As a consequence, when it does arrive (and it will), we have a lot of people who will have no idea where the risks lie. In deflation, cash is king and you can work around it somewhat. This is a risk that should be factored into your money mentality.

REINVESTMENT OF INCOME RISK. . .

Between 2010 and 2021, interest rates went down every year. This was great for borrowers, but a problem for investors. Why? Because the inability to reinvest income at commensurate rates over time eats away at your compounding return. If you reinvest assets earning a 4-5% return at 1-2%, you lose your edge over inflation.

HORIZON AND LONGEVITY RISK. . .

It's amazing to me how many people think they will either run out of money or not have enough. Investors with $10 million, $25 million, or $75 million to their names should be immune to that, but for those with less, longevity should be a high priority. An unexpected life event can completely derail your plans, and you'd be wise to be prepared. It goes back to the theory in my book *The Psychology of Staying Rich,* that cash is a must for long-term investors.

REAL ESTATE RISK. . .

While I am sure I'll get some pushback here, there is risk in real estate. Over the many years I've had people tell me how much they've made off property, I've always posed this question: *How long did you own it?* Many times, their compound returns are not all that great, even though the absolute number sounds good. Another viable question is, *What did it cost to keep?* Some investors are quick to forget the cumulative costs of maintenance, improvements, insurance, and taxes—all inevitable expenses tied to keeping up property value. There are many other ways real estate can go wrong. There are those who leverage too much because they haven't been through a downturn. That's a lesson people don't forget, as real estate is great when it's working, but a very illiquid item when it's not. There are novices who rely on recourse financing instead of non-recourse financing, not understanding joint and several liability until it's too late. And there are those who make mistakes in investing in land over buildings, misjudging locations, establishing poorly-constructed lease agreements, and disregarding times when markets are in flux or simply not what they seem.

The important thing to remember in all this is that there are a lot of risks to understand. You cannot let your money mentality—the way you feel or lean on investments—override reality.

OXBOW NOTE

Strange as it may sound, holding onto wealth often turns out to be harder for families than getting it in the first place. The majority of wealthy Americans fail to keep their fortunes in the family for more than a single generation—and many don't make it that far. If you'd like a free copy of The Psychology of Staying Rich: How to Preserve Wealth and Establish an Enduring Financial Legacy, *contact us at OxbowAdvisors.com.*

CHAPTER 5

Investing Is Hard to Learn

Financial investing is hard to learn for a lot of reasons. First, it covers a wide range of areas, each of which requires its own knowledge base and skill set. Second, much of the financial industry wants it that way, as it contributes to Wall Street's ability to sell you its products at will. Third, and perhaps most important, true investment knowledge comes from wide experience—enough to know it's a world of constant change and enough to stay steady when crazy times inevitably come.

Unfortunately, the money mentality of countless investors doesn't allow them to recognize the challenges of truly learning the field. They perceive it as something black and white, like basic math. They think if they can learn a few rules—when to add, when to subtract, when to divide and multiply—they can certainly and easily master the intricacies of investment. This is the attitude that gets people into trouble, especially people who have great confidence and great fortunes. That combination has led to some of the most devastating financial losses I've witnessed.

Each economic cycle is completely different and there is always a changing landscape of risk. If I ask the majority of investors a few questions, their answers would show very little knowledge of financial investing. It does not mean they are not smart or don't have the capacity to understand. It means they haven't given this complex field the amount of time and attention it deserves. This is doubly true of stocks, a field in which almost every aspect is foreign to most people because it's all so intangible.

Real estate investing is easier to grasp. You can see and feel your investment. You know the price and the way the product is built. You know the lease requirements and ways to eliminate a lot of risk. You can reduce your risk by buying insurance, and there are great tax benefits. There is no investment in which you *can't* lose money, but it's harder to do in real estate. But people in real estate tend to forget about costs of upkeep when they sing its praises. Another downside is the most obvious one: real estate isn't freely liquid. When times are bad it can be hard to find buyers.

Stocks on the other hand have an aura of mystery. They are harder to grasp. When it comes to what they buy in stocks, most people buy what they're familiar with. They go to Walmart, shop at Lulu Lemon, order from Amazon, or ship via Fedex—and so they look to those familiar names when they buy stocks. But does a corporation's role in your life really give you any insight into its investment value? Probably not. You see it go higher or lower without understanding all the elements involved. General Electric was $31 per share in 2016 and by mid-2018 had fallen to $16 per share. The average person, no matter how smart, looks at that kind of relative price difference for a stock associated with a familiar company and thinks, *I need to buy*. Few suspected it would drop to $6 per share in less than a year—but that's exactly what happened. This is what is most frustrating about finance—most people are playing a high-stakes game for which they don't actually know the rules.

I met Wall Street icon Roy Neuberger when he was 102 years old, and I often think of his advice to anybody thinking of delving into finance. He said, "Before you begin studying companies for investment, study yourself."

Warren Buffett took the sentiment a step further, saying, "The most important quality for investors is temperament, not intellect."

If you don't have a patient, steady, and thoughtful temperament, if you're not willing to listen and learn, then think twice about investing in stocks. Most business owners understand their own companies, and in many cases thoroughly understand entire industries. They are the preeminent experts in their own fields. The mistake these powerful and successful people make time and again is believing their industry-specific knowledge somehow applies to investing in stocks and bonds. Sadly, it doesn't work that way, and most of them won't recognize even the hint of a problem until they start losing money.

We at Oxbow have worked with business owners after selling their companies for decades. This group has proven themselves the very best at building companies, selling them, and reaping cash benefits. When they cash out and look ahead to what they want to do next, they are on top of the world. When it comes to risk, however, they're often standing up there with their toes over the edge. They know everything about the field they just left, and very little about the investment world they're about to enter. Many are looking for returns commensurate with what they earned in the business; and they imagine those returns will largely be achieved without volatility. Neither of these things is guaranteed—or likely.

For this reason, my advice before you dive in is to take a break. Go slow. Get to know the landscape. If it helps, think about it in terms of the business you left behind and how you'd proceed cautiously and methodically into any new venture with that. You wouldn't just get up one morning and decide to sell a completely different product, to an untested market, using unproven vendors, relying on a new management team. You wouldn't dream of it. I suggest you apply the same kind of care and due diligence into your research about how you want to invest and who you trust to help as you would put into a business expansion.

OXBOW NOTE

If you are a first-generation wealth earner who's just sold your company, this is a critical time in your financial life and an area of specialization for us at Oxbow Advisors. For free copies of more of our books about this make-or-break time, contact us at OxbowAdvisors.com.

CHAPTER 6

Finding Risk-Appropriate Investment Guidance

The first step in figuring out where and how to invest any newly liquid fortune is accepting that once you're *out* of the business, investing *becomes* the business. When you come into newly liquid wealth, your primary professional function becomes ensuring your financial security—not just for the coming fiscal term, but for life. If you're like most investors, this applies not just to your own life, but to the next generations of your family. More than anything, most wealthy investors want to ensure they can create a long-term safety net for their children and grandchildren.

What NOT To Do:

- *"Trust the formula."* It's a common Wall Street fallacy that investment groups have a fool-proof formula for your investments—x percentage in b stocks, y percentage in c bonds, etc. Think about it: If it was that easy, why would you need a firm? Remember, investing is both art and science, all of it complicated by deeply-held personal priorities and risk tolerances. Anybody that tells you there's a one-size-fits-all formula for doing it right is blowing hot air.

- *"Go with the big name."* It's a funny thing in the investment business that many of the biggest firms aren't so much famous as infamous. The things we know some of them for are questionable guidance, staggering losses, and scandals. The biggest of the Wall Street firms have their hands in too many pots to prioritize the assets of the individual investor. The same people who are underwriting equity and debt offerings for public companies should not be deciding (or even recommending) who invests in them.

- *"Let your advisors do the thinking."* There's a critical line between being overconfident in your investment knowledge and being too trusting of someone else's. The job of an investment firm is to understand your needs, your priorities and your comfort level with risk—and then guide your investments accordingly. Anybody telling you to just sit back and watch your money grow without taking the time to get to know you and what's important to you first has simply got their hand in your pocket. You are not a silent partner in your investments. This is all the more reason to be sure you understand your own money mentality before you partner with anyone to help execute your preferences.

What You Should Do:

- *Do your research.* Choose your investment advisors the same way you'd choose any other employee, vendor, or partner. Vet the individual and the company. Ask questions. Look at the records. Request (and expect to receive) references. This selection may be one of the most important financial decisions you ever make, so take it seriously.

- *Demand experience.* There's an old saying about not asking a boy to do a man's job. Ditto a girl for a woman's. Yes, you want an educated team advising you on your investments. But no number of Ivy League MBAs is equal to the schooling that comes from experience, and that's doubly true when you're dealing with vast sums of money. At Oxbow, we have advisors as old as 86 and as young as 23, covering the whole gamut of experience and working together to share it. The young advisors who major investment firms frequently put on the front lines have not been through enough risk scenarios to be able to help you find clarity on your volatility tolerance. They're still textbook investors, figuring out their own money mentality. They certainly aren't ready to tell you yours.

- *Expect time and questions.* The only way an advisor can get in tune with your money mentality is to spend time understanding where you're coming from and what's important to you. Most investors do not fit the Wall Street profile and so won't have their needs met by any pre-determined formulas. The fact is, your advisors should take the time to identify your needs, and then work to them. It should never be the other way around.

- *Listen.* Once you've put in the time and energy to find a reputable, knowledgeable firm that takes the time to get to know you, *listen* to the people you found worthy of your trust. I can't tell you how many times I've seen bull-headed investors who are on their right path panic and sell at the bottom or get too aggressive and end up going all in at the top when good, seasoned advisors not only asked them to reconsider, but laid out clear strategic and logical reasons for doing so. If you work with an individual or firm that understand and respects your particular risk tolerance, you owe it to yourself to tune in to their advice.

OXBOW NOTE

First-generation wealth earners need to constantly guard against schemes designed to separate them from their wealth. These tests of your judgment don't always come in the form of shady characters with questionable reputations. Many show up polished, with the sheen of Wall Street on them. Just remember the caveat about buyer beware. If you'd like a free copy of Oxbow's analysis of the scams designed to separate you from your money, **Wall Street Lies: 5 Myths to Keep Your Cash in Their Game,** *contact us at OxbowAdvisors.com.*

CHAPTER 7

Critical Questions and Answers

oney is one of our most powerful emotional triggers, and
few things are as stressful to people as their finances. They
are a major cause of divorces, business breakups, family
problems, and sleepless nights, and they can equally be a source of
security, freedom, and pride. With that in mind, investors should
be doing all they can to understand their money mentality—how
they feel, how they view investment, and why.

Most investors never think about some of the most important questions that relate to their money mentality. At Oxbow, we
spend enormous amounts of time on this. The standard Wall Street
questionnaire looks about the same for every firm—which makes

sense because most of those firms see investors as interchangeable. You don't have to look far to see that this assumption is false—to recognize that money mentality is profoundly influenced by factors that can't be explained with formulas or mere numbers. Think about the people closest to you—siblings, business partners, and friends. Odds are you can easily identify someone whose socio-economic profile is similar to yours, but who doesn't share your financial priorities and outlook. On paper, you need the same things. In practice, that's not how good financial management works, because money mentality is highly personal.

Any financial advising professional you consider should be quick to acknowledge what they don't know at the outset or your relationship. They don't know what you want or don't want relative to money. They don't know how wealth and the burdens and privileges that come with it make you feel, or how you respond to those feelings. They don't know how you see yourself contributing in the long term to your extended family's finances or to charitable organizations that are important to you. They don't know if you intend to live beneath your means or if you want to be a big spender. They don't know if you're driven by a fear of failure, a need to win, or some other deep-seated emotion or combination of them. They don't know if life has ever humbled you, or if that's still in your future (because all of us get there sooner or later).

At Oxbow, we start our relationships by recognizing what we don't know, and then we ask questions to help us get at the crux of who you are and what you need. We realize we need insight into these things to provide good guidance. With that in mind, below are some of the topics we explore, and why. The questions are examples, not a boilerplate, as we customize our approach to each investor. I think of them like a financial personality test—a series of inquiries and responses that help create a snapshot of your history, present situation, and money mentality. Once we have that baseline, we can start a dialogue about the future—what you want and how best to get you there.

No matter where you currently stand in the investment world, you can gain perspective by thinking about the implications of your answers to these inquiries. Even if you're just doing a run-through at home, they are a valuable tool in getting to the core of *knowing thyself.*

QUESTIONS ABOUT POSITION

- Do you know how much your accounts made as a percent last year in total?

- Do you know how many accounts you have?

These questions help get at some bedrock information about your investing: your accounts. The factual answers matter, but so does your on-the-spot knowledge of them. They're indicative of whether you're closely involved in your investment situation or perhaps keeping some distance.

- Is there a percentage in your head that would satisfy you in terms of annual return?

For some people, this is a straightforward question with a straightforward answer. For others, answers hint at something deeper—like dissatisfaction with current returns, determination to outpace any reasonable goal, or even a lack of understanding that the number one goal of investment is to maintain buying power. You can do it a lot of ways, but if you can't stay ahead of inflation, you fail the biggest test. Why? On average, inflation has run around 3% over the past century. If you compound that figure over ten years and don't earn returns to balance it, then your money may lose a full third of its buying power over just ten years. That's why you don't keep money under the mattress, and it's why almost every investor must set a first and critical investment goal at ensuring continued buying power. Maintaining the power of the money you have is far more important than making more.

- Have you ever had a loss greater than 20% of your net worth?

People who answer yes to this question have had their nerve tested. Most have had their egos adjusted as well. Typically, the experience wakes them up to the realities of their risk tolerance and the absolute need to separate the "bulletproof" money that provides their long-term security from funds that can be risked on a chance of bigger gains. People who are shocked at the mere idea of this question likely haven't experienced a hard downturn yet and undergone the resulting reality check about their money mentality. They may still be feeling go-big-or-go-home about the stock market, not fully comprehending that the true test of risk tolerance is loss.

If this has happened to you more than once, it's time to take a hard look at your strategy. You are likely risking too much. If you're not clear on the *why* or *how* of it—or if you believe your money is just at the whim of external forces—seek a trustworthy advisor. There's a good chance what you're doing is not strategic investing at all; it's obscenely expensive and misguided on-the-job training.

QUESTIONS ABOUT ENGAGEMENT

- Do you check the stock market every day?

- On vacation, what is the longest you go without checking the market?

These questions can help investors gain some perspective on investing's place in their lives. Is it a useful tool? Is it a source of aggravation? Is it something you obsess about? Or do you feel confident enough that your investment choices are solid that you don't need a steady feed of information from the markets to function?

- Do you look back at things you sold and calculate 'what if'?

On the surface, this is a basic yes/no inquiry. In practice, for many people it packs an emotional punch. I have seen and heard responses that were flaming angry and others that were heavy with regret. If you've already made your fortune, your finances shouldn't be able to make you feel like that. If they do, either your investment choices or your money mentality (most likely both) need attention.

Losses happen—to everyone. If you make a mistake, make it a learning moment. I've been doing this for a very long while, and I still have my own learning moments from time to time. They're a reminder to be humble and stay open to new ideas and lessons.

- What was your happiest time related to investing?
- What was your most depressing?

When I ask about the happiest time, part of what I want to know is if you've got any. For some people, engagement in investment is always stressful. Like going to the dentist, it's just something they have to do. For some people, investment is about chasing the thrill of "winning" and their answers reflect that. These answers speak to both attitude and philosophy.

When we talk about the most depressing time, what I really want to know is how you handled that. Were your assets so low that you were scared of running out? Were you gutted by losing 30%? Did you panic during a market plunge and sell? Did your fear of missing out drive you to overinvest at the top and then suffer losses? No matter what happened, how do you feel about it now? The investment world is not a place to dwell on what you should have or could have done. It's a place where you learn from your mistakes and move on. If you're hung up on the past, that may color your money mentality more than any other single factor in your life.

QUESTIONS ABOUT MOTIVATION

- Do you worry about not having enough money?

I've worked with people who have a couple million dollars who feel happy and secure; and I've worked with people who have a billion dollars and can't sleep at night because they still don't think they're set. These perceptions are mental and emotional, but they don't have any grounding in reality. If you've sold a business for substantial wealth and are shifting your attention to the investment world, it's time for a reality check. You have everything you need. Now you have to hang on to it and maintain its buying power. No pressure to "make it" should ever drive you to bad choices, or to stress over money problems that don't need to exist.

- What does your perfect quality of life look like?

Inevitably, part of the answer to this question is based on achieving (or preserving) true security—for the investor and for the investor's family. If you have children and grandchildren, you want to put a big net under them for the rest of their lives to keep them financially safe. This is human nature, plain and simple. I advise investors to do this carefully, though—to remember that work has its own rewards and their heirs will be happier and safer if they can achieve self-sufficiency than if they cannot. If you're interested in reading more about this topic, my books *Rich Kids, Broke Kids* and *The Psychology of Staying Rich* both explore them in detail. Beyond the shared basic interest of security, though, people have widely different priorities, and this question is a tool that helps you start getting at them and understanding the role that money mentality plays.

My advice on the subject is this: Your life is comprised of interwoven threads. Money is one, but it's very thin on its own. The other threads—mental and physical health, relationships with family and friends, the work you do, the legacy you build—they tie in to create something substantial and valuable. When you picture your perfect life, look at all your threads. This question is about who you are, not what you have.

- Do your compare your net worth to friends? To colleagues? To adversaries?

Some people are born competitors. This is a common mindset among entrepreneurs and successful business people—even after they leave the industry. A lifetime of looking for any competitive edge in business doesn't just fade away when you sell your company. Many times it shifts to other aspects of your life. A healthy place to take it is the golf course. Less healthy? Wealth comparisons. I'll never get used to encountering grown men and women with independent wealth—truly on top of the world—who remain focused on being the best and having the most.

No matter what you've got, there's always going to be somebody who has more. Instead of choosing to measure your worth by looking at someone else's; instead of being motivated by winning, be motivated by something internal. Are you happy? Do you have everything you need? Do you have fulfilling things to do with your time? Are you comfortable with your wealth and your investment choices? All those are things that matter. For those who can't let competition go, I'd share a quote from legendary investor Charlie Munger. "Envy is a really stupid sin," he said, "because it's the only one you could never possibly have any fun at."

Don't waste your energy on the stupid sin. Focus on what you have and how to make the most of it. When you're struggling with this, do something to help you shift your attention from what you don't have to what you do have. In entrepreneurship, in shepherding a business, and in investment, people typically set goals and measure. When we fall short, the simple view is,

I missed it. But that's not the whole picture. What *did* you get done? Sit down and write out your accomplishments, successes, the connections you made and the things you made happen. Look at what you have.

- Do you have a number in mind that you and your spouse would like to leave to your children or charity at your death?

Most wealthy people think about the subject of legacy often and deeply. They do have a number in mind. Some go so far as to feel guilty for spending their hard-earned wealth. If you wrestle with this, I suggest you don't. Live well. Enjoy your life. Support your kids, but know that true support is more than a trust fund. It's encouraging and expecting productivity. It's recognizing and respecting individuals for who they are, not for what you want them to be. If you have a charitable interest, start being of benefit to it now as well as planning for the future. I speak from both personal experience and from hearing wealthy investors over decades report that these are things that have enriched their lives.

QUESTIONS ABOUT TOLERANCE

- Do you gamble on anything? Las Vegas, football games, poker or horses?

The thing about the gambling is this: There are a lot of people who have a taste for it. If you do it for recreation, maybe that's just in fun. But maybe it indicates a high tolerance for risk and a high drive to "win." In the investment world, these can be dangerous qualities. Does the urge to roll the dice subside when you leave the table? If not (or if you're not sure), this is a key piece of your money mentality, and being aware of it will help you keep it in check.

- Can you easily sell an asset at a loss?

- Do stock losses irritate you?

- Have you ever thought about selling out when stock markets are low?

These questions all get at a baseline of risk tolerance, examining whether you fundamentally understand that it's all-but-impossible to gain in market investing without experiencing loss—that loss is part of the process. It looks at whether you take these investing realities too much to heart, and whether you might be prone to panic. Each of these is a piece of the puzzle of your money mentality, and each tells you something you should be mindful of as you make investment choices.

QUESTIONS ABOUT PHILOSOPHY

- Do you see success in terms of wealth levels?

- Is making money your purpose for investing?

The purpose of investing should be to meet your needs for income and to keep the buying power of your money intact for your whole life. If these questions bring you straight to goals that have to do with beating a particular manager or index, it may be time to revisit your philosophy and assess whether your money mentality is bringing unnecessary tension, aggression, or anxiety to your life. The way you view money is a reflection of your life philosophy. Taking the time to understand it can steer you towards wisdom, and away from short-sighted tactics that could ultimately cost you both cash and self-esteem.

OXBOW NOTE

Because this is such a critical issue to wealth preservation, at Oxbow we excel not just in helping families with money but in structuring arrangements so that money doesn't disappear in the next generation. For more information about how to approach legacy planning in your own family, contact us at OxbowAdvisors.com.

CHAPTER 8

Regrets and Second Chances

REGRETS, I'VE HAD A FEW . . .

Just like Sinatra sang, we all have some regrets—especially when it comes to investing. Holding a losing stock too long and selling a winning stock too soon are two of the most prevalent. Over the last 40 years I have witnessed unbelievable regret in many forms from investors. These are among the most common. Odds are at least one will be all-too-familiar.:

- *I can't believe I didn't sell . . .* In many market cycles, I've witnessed hot stocks completely overwhelm average investors. The way it plays out is ironic. They buy the stock, and over the cycle it explodes to new highs and great profits. Great news, except the "victory" becomes an ego booster disproportionate to the investor's competence. They get in their heads that they've mastered investing, even if it's a one-stock one-off. When I advise "You should probably sell some of that and book the gains," it inevitably falls on deaf ears. In the 80s, it was Circuit City and Toys "R" Us. In the early 90s, it was Coca-Cola and Masco. Then the tech stocks came into play—Cisco Systems, Yahoo, AOL, and many others. In today's world, it may be Tesla or Facebook. They all rose, and they all stopped. Countless investors beat themselves up in the end because they didn't understand that nothing goes up forever.

- *I can't believe I sold so soon . . .* The flip side of the investor above is the one that sells after a small gain, thinking it will trade back. This goes on all the time. A person identifies a great company and makes a purchase. It goes up 20% and they sell out. Three years later it is up 300% and they have regret. In many studies, it's been revealed that the average investor could improve returns by selling their losers and keeping their winners. Sadly, most people tend to think about what a stock has already done instead of what it will do in the future.

- *I can't believe I didn't go my own way . . .* One of the worst things investors do is compare themselves to others. Sitting around a lunch or dinner table with friends, egos start to fly, bragging starts, and the game of *what I got* and *what I missed* starts. Comparing yourself to other investors—especially when you're only hearing the highlights—is a losing proposition. Instead of worrying about what someone else is earning, look in the mirror and figure out who you are and what matters most to you. What kind of investor should that make you? There is no Holy Grail in investing, but there are people who know their minds and their priorities. Those are the ones who sleep soundly at night and don't spend their days thinking about money. They know they're secure and well-placed—and they understand that has to be enough.

GETTING PAST REGRET

Resilient people have a few things in common. First, they understand that adversity in investing happens to everyone. Second, they understand what they control and what they don't. They know that yesterday's losses or gains are history. Lastly, they are usually grateful every day for what they do have. That puts a positive spin on every experience.

Most regret comes when investors make bad decisions and then blame themselves. There's no point in beating yourself up, so set aside that feeling. No one is perfect and everyone in the investment business has made mistakes—big ones. What separates out comfortable, confident investors from those who can't forgive themselves is what they learn from their missteps. So go forward with a little regret, but not a great weight.

DOING BETTER STARTS HERE

If you aspire to be a steadier investor, there are some common-sense measures that can help you get there. Start with these steps:

- *Really think about how much you want to tie your fortunes to stocks.* Have you considered whether you'd be okay with losing 25% of your money? Because that may be the price you pay to be in the stock market, the amount of fluctuation you must reasonably be prepared to accept. If your answer is no, then you cannot be all stock.

- *Look at the big picture.* If you've been really good at making money in the last few years, have you stopped to wonder if you'll notice when the game is over? Bear markets will eventually come—they always do. But most people take far too long to recognize it happening and change course. They don't want to mess with a "good thing."

- *Don't follow the herd.* It's easy to imagine investing as a group sport, but it is not. It is about knowing when to think independently. Investors deceive themselves when a lot of their return was either timing or just plain luck. It happens all the time—not just to a few outliers, but to vast swaths of investors who get caught up in the buzz or the news or the optics of a company. It happened to the buyers of companies like Polaroid in the 60s, Coca-Cola in the 80s, Nortel in the 90s, Enron in the 2000s, and even Tesla in 2020. Do you think it's a coincidence so many people fell in love with these companies and others like them and lost? Or were investors led to them, to over-paying and over-investing? Don't let Wall Street or anyone else charm you into thinking any company can do no wrong, because they are all fallible, and nothing goes up forever.

- *Know that timing is relative.* One of the biggest and most common mistakes novice investors make is thinking they're ahead when they're actually behind. Sounds unlikely, I know, but this is how it works: Investor A gets a good feeling about Company Z's stock. The company is solid, conditions for future growth are ripe, and the name or the product or a theory about what happens next catches his eye—and so he makes a substantial investment in the stock. When the earnings report comes around, the company nails it, meeting or beating estimates and making a billion dollars in the quarter (sometimes many quarters in a row). Investor A waits for the stock price to soar, but instead it stays the same. Maybe it even drops. Why? Because experienced and knowledgeable investors were watching Company Z all along, were valuing the stock, were buying and selling. By the time Investor A felt compelled to purchase, all the positive factors that caught his eye were already priced into the stock.

The fact most investors don't understand is that whatever is going on right now in the market means very little to the future. They use common sense to try and make current events match up with which way to go in investing. That can be a costly error.

- *Trust your plan.* Last and most importantly, know that the right investment plan for you is one that you can follow, not one that someone else tells you to follow. Managing your levels of greed, panic, and insecurity all come back to investor behavior. And all investor behavior comes back to understanding yourself and being confident in your choices. You have to have confidence to sell when the mood is optimistic. You have to have confidence to buy when everyone around you is despondent and wouldn't dream of it.

More often than not, the way you find and keep this confidence is by working with an advisor who respects and understands your priorities, pairing them with a depth and breadth of experience and knowledge about smart, steady investment. The primary way to overcome regret is to have a system and stick with it. So set levels on what you invest in every area and stay with them.

SEPARATE WHO YOU ARE FROM WHAT YOU HAVE

Have you ever thought about what it would be like to start over? What would happen if you woke up tomorrow, back at the beginning? It's not a bad way to put your feelings about volatility in perspective. I think about it sometimes—in fact, I make a point of it. It reminds me that building self-esteem on money is like constructing a house on sand. It's a shifting foundation and it's one that discounts all the personal qualities that truly define worth.

What would I think if it happened to me? I'd start with, *Well, I've been here before.*

I grew up poor. I don't want to go back, but if it happened I'd keep it together and set about the process of getting on my feet. More importantly, I'd still be the same man I was the day before—someone who knows he'll be okay. The *why* of that realization is simple, or impossible, depending on your relationship with your wealth. Either you are able to separate your identity from your money, or you still have work to do on that score.

This isn't about whether you're ever going to see a back-to-square-one scenario. If you're smart and steady, separate your no-touch security money from your invest-and-see money, and don't put yourself in the company of unscrupulous advisors, you're not going there. But the crux of your money mentality is tied up in the question of who you are without it. Maybe you're a parent, a spouse, an investor, a friend, and a traveler. Maybe you see yourself as generous or hardworking, clever or driven, or a maverick who thinks with total independence. You were likely all those things before you made your fortune. And you'd still have those qualities without it. People who can't make that distinction get into trouble, because their money mentality includes a kind of desperation to define and continue to prove themselves.

Whatever it is you have to do to feel okay as a person separate from your money—whether it's work or workouts, having a close hand in your investments or keeping some distance, or any other personal touchstone—know that valuable process is helping to keep your feet on the ground. If you can align your investments accordingly, you can spend less time worrying, and more time feeling comfortable in the security that comes with wealth. When you get there, you can count yourself among the Steady Eds instead of one of the more volatile investment types.

OXBOW NOTE

For more on the subject of raising families who aren't tainted by wealth, you can request a free copy of my book Rich Kids, Broke Kids: The Failure of Traditional Estate Planning *at OxbowAdvisors.com.*

If You Ask Only One Question

I f I had to distill everything in these pages and on the topics of risk and money mentality down to one question, it would be this: *What is your choking point?*

Everyone has one, and the number is often arbitrary—not tied to specific needs, but to emotions and personal perceptions. Whether your fortune tops $5 million, $50 million, or $500 million, deep down you know this number and live with it. It's the point at which you say to yourself, "This is the bottom." It's the invisible line you're not willing to cross with your assets, the floor of your risk tolerance.

It's good practice to revisit this number from time to time, to assess just how close to it your current circumstances could bring you. Why? Because there are times in every century of investing when major setbacks or declines come along like tidal waves and wipe out those who are in too deep. These events can take many forms—from wars and weather events to disease and political shake-ups. They can wipe out trillions of dollars in assets in a matter of days or even hours. Like hundred-year floods, these rare events don't always have to be widely spaced from one another—sometimes they come in quick succession and further swamp the unprepared.

Most of these events will eventually recede or altogether end, making room for recovery and new gains. Steady investors will keep their heads and feel confident that even in crisis, even if the market shuts down, they remain shareholders of companies that have value independent of the stock exchange.

But there are always some investors who won't recover on the other side of catastrophic financial moments because they risked beyond that critical point of no return.

Wall Street does not tell you any of this because they don't care about your choking point. They will always have a standard allocation and just sell you on that allocation. What's left out of that formula—and equally out of moments when the public gets caught up in speculation—is simply the number one thing in successful investing: risk management.

Regularly asking yourself, "What is my choking point?" and

maintaining awareness of that number will give you a solid and realistic frame of reference for how you invest. It'll help steer you to investments that fit your money mentality. A funny thing happens when you pull that off, one best summed up by author Morgan Housel in his book *The Psychology of Money.* He writes, "More than I want big returns, I want to be financially unbreakable. And if I'm unbreakable I actually think I'll get the biggest returns, because I'll be able to stick around long enough for compounding to work." This wisdom is at the core of good investment sense and a healthy money mentality. If you want to truly be unbreakable, you can't put everything at risk.

About the Author

J. Ted Oakley, founder and managing partner of Oxbow Advisors, began his career in the investment industry in 1976. The Oxbow Principles and the firm's proprietary investment strategies are founded on the unique perspective he has gained during his decades-long tenure advising high-net-worth investors. Ted's investment advice provides principled guidance to investors from more than half the states in the US. He frequently counsels former business owners on protecting and wisely investing their newly liquid wealth. Ted is the author of several other books, including:

- *You Sold Your Company*

- *$20 Million and Broke*

- *The Psychology of Staying Rich*

- *Danger Time: The 2-3 Year Red Zone after Selling Your Company*

- *Rich Kids, Broke Kids: The Failure of Traditional Estate Planning*

- *Crazy Time: Surviving the First 12 Months after Selling your Company*

- *My Story*

- *Wall Street Lies: 5 Myths to Keep Your Cash in Their Game with Pat Swanson and Trey Crain*

Made in the USA
Las Vegas, NV
20 January 2023

65957139R00046